WESTRAY

WESTRAY

The Long Way Home

Chris O'Neill
&
Ken Schwartz

Talonbooks

2004

Talonbooks
P.O. Box 2076, Vancouver, British Columbia, Canada V6B 3S3
www.talonbooks.com

Typeset in New Baskerville and printed and bound in Canada.
Printed on 100% post-consumer recycled paper.

First Printing: September 2004

Westray: The Long Way Home was originally published by Blizzard Publishing, Winnipeg, Manitoba, in 1997.

Library and Archives of Canada Cataloguing in Publication
O'Neill, Chris, 1970-
Westray : the long way home / Chris O'Neill and Ken Schwartz. – 2nd ed.
A play.
ISBN 0-88922-491-9
1. Westray Mine Disaster, Plymouth, Pictou, N.S., 1992–Drama.
I. Schwartz, Ken, 1969- II. Title.
PS8579.N3866W47 2004 C812'.54 C2004-903257-7

The publisher gratefully acknowledges the financial support of the Canada Council for the Arts; the Government of Canada through the Book Publishing Industry Development Program; and the Province of British Columbia through the British Columbia Arts Council for our publishing activities.

Canadä

For the families of the twenty-six,
and those who struggled to save them.

—Chris O'Neill &
Ken Schwartz

The original version of *Westray: The Long Way Home* was produced by Two Planks and a Passion Theatre, and opened at the DeCoste Centre, in Pictou, Nova Scotia on April 21, 1995, with the following cast:

GERRY	Gordon Gammie
PAM	Allena MacDonald
ANDY	Malcolm Wilson
MARJORIE	Chris O'Neill
DAVID	Josh MacDonald

Director: Ken Schwartz
Composer: Jeff Hennessy
Stage Manager: Sarah Blenkhorn

It was later remounted, in this version, in May 2002 with the following cast:

GERRY	Ryan Rogerson
PAM	Martha Irving
ANDY	Réjean Cournoyer
MARJORIE	Francine Deschepper
DAVID	Andrew Bigelow

Director: Ken Schwartz
Composer: Jeff Hennessy
Stage Manager: Donna MacMillan

The play was based on the book *Calculated Risk: Greed, Politics, and the Westray Tragedy*, by Dean Jobb, and published by Nimbus Publishing.

Acknowledgments

Because this play was written in a workshop setting, through the theatre company of which we are artistic directors, more people were responsible for its success than would perhaps be apparent. Many thanks to Dean Jobb, whose generosity with his raw interviews and source materials was invaluable; the United Steelworkers of America, who sponsored the original production (especially Pat Van Horne and Mike Piche, who was involved in the tragedy and who gave us insight we could not have received elsewhere). The actors for the original production of this show were also very supportive, and the characters are in some important ways their creations as well as ours, and our composer, Jeff Hennessy, helped bring the show to life with his haunting music.

Without government support, we would not have been able to afford to write, and so we thank both the Canada Council and the Nova Scotia Department of Education and Culture.

Finally, we would like to express our heartfelt thanks to audience members throughout Canada who have made this play the success it has been from coast to coast.

Chris O'Neill
Ken Schwartz

In memory of Dr. Ronald Irving Carr

Scene 1

A dining room, early one morning. GERRY is sitting at the table, reading the Chronicle Herald, while PAM rushes back and forth from the kitchen, bringing in breakfast and trying to get things moving.

PAM:

(*From off*) One or two?

GERRY:

Two, please. What's an eight-letter word for unsuspicious?

PAM:

Mmm … trusting?

GERRY:

Nope. Has two L's in the middle.

PAM:

Oh, gullible. Here, eat up.

GERRY:

How about a six-letter word for playful?

PAM:

(*Calling out to her son*) Lloyd, time to get up! Frisky.

GERRY:

Perfect. How's he doing in school these days anyway? I never get to ask him.

PAM:

Lloyd? Oh, pretty well. He's finally over that biting thing, and he says the other kids aren't bothering him so much anymore.

GERRY:

(*Noticing her toast*) No more toast?

PAM:

You never want toast.

GERRY:

You never ask me.

PAM:

I never ask you because … Oh eat mine.

She notices that he has folded the paper over itself.

Don't you be screwing up the paper. You do that every morning and it drives me right out of my tree. Last week you took the puzzles to the can, and I couldn't find them for ages.

GERRY:

That's all right Pam, they're a waste of time, anyway.

PAM:

At least I don't spend my time plugging loonies into machines. You know you could actually get ahead if you didn't stop into the bar every night.

GERRY:

Maybe I just need to see a bit more of you.

He goes to spear her with a fork, and she deflects him with the newspaper.

PAM:

Don't you dare, or else you'll be eating breakfast with the dog.

ANDREW wanders in, still in pyjamas.

ANDREW:

What's going on?

GERRY:

Jesus, Andy, aren't you dressed yet? I told you I wanted to leave a bit early today.

ANDREW:

(*Looking at the eggs*) Pam, I don't like them done fancy like that at all.

PAM:

Too bad. You're late. Now get going.

ANDREW:

See the respect I get in my own house? It's a disgrace.

GERRY:

Those pyjamas are the disgrace. Where the hell did you get those homely things?

PAM:

You eat your eggs and shut your mouth. I got those for him.

GERRY:

You want me to eat with my mouth closed?

PAM:

Actually that would be an improvement over seeing your insides every time you take a bite. Honestly, you're worse than Lloyd.

ANDREW:

Speaking of Lloyd, did his teacher say anything about that biting thing? (*To GERRY*) You know he actually tore the ear right off of MacCalister's mutt. I told Mac that his dog started it, but he wouldn't listen. He wanted to test him for rabies.

GERRY:

Who? The dog, or Lloyd?

PAM:

Enough, he'll hear you. I think he did it because you two were always laughing when he did. (*To ANDREW*) You were the one who told him to bite in the first place.

ANDREW:

That's because Lizzie was biting him, and there's no way any woman's going to keep my son down!

PAM:

I'll keep you down, boy.

GERRY:

Listen, Andy, I gotta go. You want a lift or don't you? I want to get in early today.

ANDREW:

All right, all right. What's your hurry anyway? You're not usually so eager to go to work.

GERRY:

I want to leave early tonight so I can get ready for fishing tomorrow. I have to get to town before things close.

ANDREW:

Shit, that's right. Pam—

PAM:

I know, yes your gear is in the basement. Are you going to take Lloyd?

ANDREW:

Oh, God, Pam, not this time. I just want to be able to relax, and I'd have to watch him every step of the way. After four days, I need a rest. I'll do something with him on the break though, I promise.

PAM:

Well you can tell him yourself, Andrew. That's the third time you've promised to take him, and not done it. No wonder he's acting out. I gotta get him ready for school.

She leaves.

GERRY:

(*Under his breath*) Maybe it's because he's got a mother who nags at him.

PAM:

(*From off*) I heard that!

ANDREW:

What about my breakfast? Pam!

PAM:

Fix it yourself!

ANDREW:

(*Looking for food, which is now scarce*) Jesus, you've eaten us out of house and home again. We need to find you a woman.

GERRY:

I'll take yours if you're offering.

ANDREW:

I'd like to see you try. She'd eat you alive.

GERRY:

I suppose it all depends on what you're into. Look Andy, I really want to get going.

ANDREW:

Okay, just give me two minutes. You got ants in your pants or what?

GERRY:

I'm just looking forward to getting out tonight and having four glorious days on the stream. The fish jumping, cold beer, my new lure—Now get it in gear!

ANDREW:

Sure, tease me, why don't you?

ANDREW leaves the kitchen.

GERRY is now alone, and he looks around him, finds a small boy's mitt, with a baseball in it. He begins to play with it. The door opens and MARJORIE comes in behind him without him seeing her. She is dressed all in leathers. MARJORIE clears her throat.

GERRY:

Oh Jesus! (*Turns to look at her*) Who the hell are you?

MARJORIE:

Who are *you*?

GERRY:

(*Momentarily confused*) I'm Gerry. I'm a friend of Pam and Andy's.

MARJORIE:

(*Setting herself down*) Okay, so I do have the right house.

GERRY:

Can I help you?

MARJORIE:

I'm the sister.

GERRY:

Whose?

MARJORIE:

Can't you tell?

GERRY:

Not really.

MARJORIE:

I think I should take that as a compliment, but don't tell my sister.

GERRY:

Really? You and Pam are sisters? I've never heard her talk about you at … oh.

MARJORIE:

Thank you, I feel so at home already. Are you the regular welcome wagon, or are you just in training?

GERRY:

I just didn't expect to have someone come up from behind.

MARJORIE:

Well, I don't often get to come up from behind.

GERRY:

I beg your pardon?

MARJORIE:

(*Looks at him, then finally laughs*) Look, I'm sorry. I just had a really long drive, so I'm a bit punchy. Let's start over. Hello, my name is Marjorie. Pam is my sister. I'm pleased as hell to meet you.

GERRY:

I'm Gerry. Nice to meet you too. (*Looks at his watch*) Oh Jesus, I've gotta go! (*Yells to ANDREW*) Andy! Either get your butt down here in two minutes, or you're walking to work!

MARJORIE:

Well, see? Wasn't that much more pleasant?

GERRY:

Sorry. I'm driving Andy around till he gets his pick-up working again. He's always late.

MARJORIE:

Some things never change. Is Pam here?

GERRY:

Yeah, she's just getting Lloyd ready for school. He's a bit of a handful.

MARJORIE:

Is that a nice way of saying that he's an absolute monster?

GERRY:

Oh, he's really not that bad anymore. He's not biting now, anyway.

MARJORIE:

(*Pause*) I didn't know he bit.

GERRY:

Hey, where did you come from? Just now, I mean.

MARJORIE:

Vancouver. I made it here in six days straight.

GERRY:

I've never been that far west.

He goes to yell for ANDREW again, just as PAM comes bustling back into the kitchen.

Andy—

PAM:

(*Yelling back behind her*) Lloyd, wait for your lunch! Andy, can you run it out to him at the stop? Sorry, Gerry, we'll be right with you. You'd better start coming a little (*She sees MARJORIE*) earlier ... What are you doing here?

MARJORIE:

(*To GERRY*) This must be where you learned hospitality.

PAM:

What?

MARJORIE:

I'm done school. I thought I'd come visit for a while. I can go again if you don't have enough room.

PAM:

Don't you dare. I just wasn't expecting you. How did you get here?

MARJORIE:

I drove.

PAM:

I didn't know you had a car.

MARJORIE:

I don't.

PAM:

Then how ... you bought a bike.

MARJORIE:

Yup. Finally did it. Jesus, you should try it. It's amazing.

GERRY:

What kind of bike you got?

MARJORIE:

Honda 500. It's little, but it's the only one I could afford.

PAM:

Well ...

MARJORIE:

Well ...

GERRY:

Well ...

ANDREW walks in.

ANDREW:

His bus is already gone. You'll have to drop it off at school. He ... What are you doing here?

PAM:

Andy!

MARJORIE:

Oh don't give him a hard time. That's exactly what you said. Hello, Andrew. How's work?

Pause.

GERRY:

Sorry to cut short this moving reunion, but we gotta go.

ANDREW:

Yeah. I guess I'll see you later.

MARJORIE:

Pam says I can stay forever, so I guess you will.

ANDREW:

Right. Well, I might be late tonight Pam. See you later.

PAM:

Ring.

ANDREW takes off his wedding ring and hands it to her.

GERRY:

I'll see you around. Maybe we can go biking somewhere.

MARJORIE:

Cool. I'll watch for you.

GERRY and ANDREW exit.

PAM:

"Cool"?

MARJORIE:

Oh please. Do you have anything to eat? I'm starving.

PAM:

Not much. I have to go shopping today. You can have Lloyd's lunch if you want, and I can make him something else to have later.

MARJORIE:

What's in it?

PAM:

It's just a bologna sandwich. Oh, you still not eating meat?

MARJORIE:

Nope.

She looks back at PAM.

Okay, you gonna start?

PAM:

No, no. Look, it's been this long, you must be doing all right.

MARJORIE:

Thanks.

PAM:

Marjorie, why are you here?

MARJORIE:

I told you, I just felt like seeing my big sister.

PAM:

You aren't going to tell me anything, are you?

MARJORIE:

Maybe later. Now I'm going to get my stuff from the bike before it gets soaked.

MARJORIE exits.

PAM:

Here we go again.

Blackout.

Scene 2

A locker room at Westray. GERRY and ANDREW are changing into their coveralls, sitting on a bench.

ANDREW:

How much time we got?

GERRY:

'Bout five minutes.

ANDREW:

Pass me the tape.

GERRY:

She's pretty bold, isn't she?

ANDREW:

Who, Marjorie? Yeah, I suppose that's one way to put it. I could think of a few other choice words.

GERRY:

I'm getting the feeling she's not too popular at the MacInnis household.

ANDREW:

She's all right I guess. I don't dislike her, she just doesn't make it easy for anybody to like her, that's all.

GERRY:

She seems to enjoy surprising people.

ANDREW:

She likes to keep people off balance. She's always got to have the upper hand.

GERRY:

She can't be that bad, Andy. She's got a bike.

DAVID comes in to change.

ANDREW:

What are you doing here?

DAVID:

I'm recruiting for Major League Baseball.

GERRY:

Are you working "B" shift now?

DAVID:

Just today.

ANDREW:

When did you lose your mind and volunteer for this?

DAVID:

They called me last night and said they were short two men. They said I had to come in and work overtime. What am I supposed to do?

GERRY:

Say no.

DAVID:

Like you would have said no.

GERRY:

You asked me what I thought you should have done. What I would do is a totally different question.

DAVID:

How much time we got?

ANDREW:

About five minutes.

He passes DAVID the tape.

Who you filling in for?

DAVID:

Billy Caan.

GERRY:

Billy's sick is he?

DAVID:

No. He's gone.

GERRY:

What?

DAVID:

He quit on Tuesday and packed his bags. He's on a train to Alberta, probably.

ANDREW:

Billy quit? (*Pause*) Son of a bitch.

GERRY:

That's three in a month.

ANDREW:

Sonofabitch.

GERRY:

Who could blame him? That cave-in shook him up pretty bad.

ANDREW:

Billy Caan. He's been mining coal longer than any of us.

Pause.

GERRY:

You decided how you're going to vote tomorrow?

ANDREW:

You know my vote.

DAVID:

What're you voting?

ANDREW:

You're joking.

DAVID:

No, I wanna know.

ANDREW:

Let me put it to you this way. The miners up in Cape Breton would like nothing better than for all of us to join their union. One big happy family. Brotherhood and all that crap. And then one day, we'll all wake up, and our jobs will be gone, and our union will be saying, "Sorry lads, we done our best ..." Don't you read the paper? You really think those guys want this mine to keep running? They want to bury us, is what they want to do. It's like a bunch of sheep joining the Wolf Union.

GERRY:

I'm getting the feeling that you'rc voting no.

DAVID:

(*To GERRY*) How are you voting?

Pause.

GERRY:

I haven't decided yet.

ANDREW:

What about you, Squirt?

DAVID:

I dunno.

ANDREW:

Jesus, this inspires a great deal of confidence. Well, I'll see you ladies on the truck.

ANDREW leaves.

DAVID:

You think he's right?

GERRY:

He could be. The union might be more trouble than it's worth. Maybe we're just fooling ourselves, thinking they'll fix everything for us. I dunno.

DAVID:

At this point I'd settle for crappers underground. If the union gets us a johnny on the spot, I'm there.

GERRY:

We demand crappers with dignity! That isn't very catchy.

DAVID:

As long as I get a toilet …

Fade.

SCENE 3

In Pam and Andrew's dining room, later the same day. MARJORIE is cleaning up, and humming to herself. PAM walks in, with groceries.

PAM:

Hi.

MARJORIE:

Oh, hi. Do you need a hand?

PAM:

Thanks, Margie. Actually that's all there is.

MARJORIE:

Did Lloyd get his lunch all right?

PAM:

Yeah, he was a lot happier with the burger I got him than he would have been with his bologna sandwich.

MARJORIE:

I bet.

Pause.

PAM:

You cleaned everything up. Thanks.

MARJORIE:

No problem. You know me, I like to clean.

PAM:

Hardly! Don't you remember the fights we used to have over our room?

MARJORIE:

Well, I like to clean *now.*

PAM:

Well, I think getting out on your own probably helped for that. Things get crazy around here, and when Andrew's not working he's off fishing or hunting, and I'm left with Lloyd. A lot of stuff doesn't get done.

MARJORIE:

I noticed. There was some weird stuff in that fridge.

PAM:

Are you going to stay?

MARJORIE:

Well, I wouldn't mind, if you actually could use a hand. You know, I wouldn't want to be a burden.

PAM:

Oh please.

MARJORIE:

All right. But I can help, you know. I can cook, if you don't mind some vegetarian, and I can even do laundry, but I do draw the line at free babysitting. I don't think I want to be responsible for Lloyd.

PAM:

I'm sure he'd love to spend some time with you. Not that you'd have to babysit, but if you just wanted to get to know him a bit better, I think that would be great.

MARJORIE:

I'm not real comfortable with kids.

PAM:

What? You always used to do fine with babysitting.

MARJORIE:

That's 'cause I bribed the kids. I brought them chocolate bars, so they would say nice things about me. I tried that with some boyfriends, but it never worked.

PAM:

Well, I think you'd be fine, but all right. It is after all, my job.

MARJORIE:

Oh, so is Andrew paying you now?

PAM:

Hardly, you're back in Nova Scotia, dear. It's an honour and a duty. How long you been away from home, anyway?

MARJORIE:

Not long enough.

PAM:

Well, there are some days when I wouldn't mind getting out more, but until Lloyd grows up a bit, I can't see it. I don't believe that if you have a kid you should be giving it to someone else to raise.

MARJORIE:

(*Quietly*) Some people can't help it.

PAM:

Well then they shouldn't have babies.

MARJORIE:

You own this house?

PAM:

Not yet. We'll have it paid off in another ten years.

MARJORIE:

So Andrew likes it here?

PAM:

Of course! After being away for so long, we wanted to come home.

MARJORIE:

You could have come to visit me in Toronto when I was there. I would have liked that.

PAM:

That's not what you said when you left.

MARJORIE:

Oh, that's all done now. I missed you.

PAM:

I missed you too. I could have used your help just after Lloyd was born. Andy was still away, and Dad tried to help, but he always disappeared whenever I fed Lloyd.

MARJORIE:

You breast fed?

PAM:

Yeah. You should have seen Dad's face the first time I opened my shirt. I thought he would have a heart attack!

MARJORIE:

I swear I don't know how we were conceived. Can you imagine how grim *that* honeymoon must have been?

PAM:

I'm just glad they managed it. Otherwise, I wouldn't be sitting here, not doing anything. I have to get going.

MARJORIE:

Pam …

PAM:

Yeah?

MARJORIE:

It's stupid.

PAM:

Well I don't know that. What is it?

MARJORIE:

(*Pause*) Are you happy?

PAM:

Yeah, I am. I know what we're working towards, and I can see it happening. Andy's got a good job. Are you?

MARJORIE:

Me, happy? Of course not.

PAM:

Well, as long as you're happy about it. Now I gotta get going. You okay in Lloyd's little bed? We'll put him in the other room on the air mattress.

MARJORIE:

Yeah, it's great. I'm not expecting any company.

PAM:

If you are, I want to be the first to know.

MARJORIE:

You always are, sister dear.

PAM:

Well then it must have been awful dry out there in Vancouver.

Fade.

Scene 4

Gerry's front yard. GERRY is working on his Harley. MARJORIE enters from behind and watches quietly for a few seconds.

MARJORIE:

Hi.

GERRY:

(*Startled*) Oh jeez. You scared the hell out of me.

MARJORIE:

Sorry.

GERRY:

It's okay, no harm done.

MARJORIE:

Nobody told me you had a Harley.

GERRY:

That's surprising. My Harley is my most charming attribute.

MARJORIE:

(*Absorbed in the Harley*) You can say that again …

GERRY:

Actually, you weren't supposed to agree with me there. See, that was an opening line which would allow you to say, "No, no you're …" and then you could compliment me …

Pause. MARJORIE stares at the bike and says nothing.

Yeah, it is a nice bike, isn't it?

MARJORIE:

How long have you had it?

GERRY:

About six years, now. I'm going to have to put it away soon. I suppose if I lived in Vancouver I could drive myself silly all year long.

MARJORIE:

I suppose you could.

Pause. GERRY and MARJORIE speak at once.

GERRY:

What are you—

MARJORIE:

How long have you—

BOTH:

Sorry. You first.

GERRY:

No, you.

MARJORIE:

Go ahead.

GERRY:

Okay. So, the thing is, I was wondering ... um, I was going to ... ahhh ... um ... What are you—

MARJORIE:

Yes.

GERRY:

Yes, what?

MARJORIE:

Yes, I'd like to go out on a date.

GERRY:

Oh, you were going to ask me the same thing!

MARJORIE:

No.

GERRY:

Oh.

MARJORIE:

I was going to ask you if you've known Andy for a long time.

GERRY:

(*Earnestly*) Sometimes it feels like forever. We've been working together for about ten years, off and on. Forest Hill, Gays River.

MARJORIE:

So you're best friends, then?

GERRY:

I never thought about it that way. I guess that's true, though. I suppose—Why are you asking me these questions?

MARJORIE:

I've been away from home a long time. I'm having a little trouble figuring out where I fit in around here. I thought you might have talked about it with him ... Never mind, this is stupid.

GERRY:

No, it's not stupid. I think ... I think they don't know what to think. You've been away for so long, and they haven't heard a word, and one morning you're on the doorstep.

MARJORIE:

Better late than never.

GERRY:

I think they're glad you're here, really ... I think they just need some time, that's all.

MARJORIE:

That's not what Andy said, is it?

GERRY:

No. He didn't *say* that, but I could tell that's how he felt.

MARJORIE:

Well I guess I asked the right guy then.

Pause.

So ... Aren't you going to ask me?

GERRY:

'Bout what?

MARJORIE:

About why I came home.

GERRY:

I wasn't going to, no.

MARJORIE:

Good. So where are we going, is it tonight?

GERRY:

Ahh … how about tomorrow night. Bowling?

MARJORIE:

You're kidding.

GERRY:

Why, what's tomorrow?

MARJORIE:

Nothing … that would be great. Bowling would be great.

GERRY:

Good.

MARJORIE:

On one condition.

GERRY:

Name it.

MARJORIE:

Pick me up on this bike?

Fade.

Scene 5

Pam and Andrew's kitchen, late at night. ANDREW walks in slowly, setting down his lunch box on the kitchen table, wincing as he lowers himself to sit. He opens the box and begins to inspect the contents, chooses a sandwich, and begins eating it. PAM enters. She has obviously been asleep.

PAM:

What are you doing?

ANDREW:

Eating lunch. How do they get the olives in the meat slices?

PAM:

Andy, you have to take better care of yourself. You have to eat lunch.

ANDREW:

We didn't have a lunch break today.

PAM:

You say that every day.

ANDREW:

Well then it shouldn't surprise you anymore.

PAM:

A twelve-hour shift and they don't give you a lunch break. How am I supposed to believe that?

ANDREW:

Exhibit "A."

He holds up his sandwich.

PAM:

Well if they don't give you a lunch break why don't you just take one?

ANDREW:

(*Seriously*) Because my boss has got a stack of applications this high from people who would gladly work twelve hours straight without any kind of break—in my place.

PAM:

Why don't you just talk to somebody about it? I don't—

ANDREW:

It's not that simple. (*Pause*) The boys think the Mineworkers might come around again.

PAM:

You're not thinking you voted the wrong way, are you?

ANDREW:

No. (*Pause*) Maybe. Are you happy?

PAM:

Why is everybody asking me that?

ANDREW:

Are you?

PAM:

This is what we've been working so hard for, isn't it? We don't have to move, you've got steady work …

ANDREW:

Yeah, that's true.

PAM:

But what?

ANDREW:

How long would it take us to pay this house off? Could we do it faster than we are now?

PAM:

I suppose so, I haven't really thought about it. Andy, tell me what's going on.

ANDREW:

How fast?

PAM:

I don't know. Five years, maybe. But why should we? That mine will be open at least ten years, maybe more. They just gave you a raise, for heaven's sake …

ANDREW:

They gave me a raise because we told the union to take a hike. Just tell me if you think the house could be ours in five years, honest opinion.

PAM:

Why?

ANDREW:

Because I'm not going to be able to stay ten years. Not at Westray. It's bad down there, Pam. It isn't like Forest Hill or Gays River. This is a different thing altogether. It used to be fun, there used to be a … a thrill to it. Now … (*Pause*) There's no fun anymore, Pam. All I think about from the minute I get there is how long it is till quitting time. I turned down overtime three times this week.

PAM:

So that's it, then? The thrill is gone, and so you're moving on. Did you ever stop to think about what's going to happen to us if you leave this job? We have a home here. For the first time in our lives, we have a home.

ANDREW:

I know, Pam …

PAM:

How? How would you know when you're never here? Every spare minute you're gone. Lloyd misses you desperately. You pay the bills and sleep in your bed but you're not here, Andy. I feel like I'm living with a stranger.

Pause.

Is there somebody else?

Pause. ANDREW begins to laugh.

That wasn't a funny question.

ANDREW:

Yes it was.

PAM:

Well what am I supposed to think? You've had me worried sick.

ANDREW:

Look, I don't want to lose this, Pam. There's nothing to worry about. I'm just not happy working down there. I'm not saying I'll leave tomorrow … I won't leave until you say it's okay. I just want to know what has to be done, and I'll do it.

PAM:

You can start with getting to know your son again.

Pause.

ANDREW:

I suppose I deserve that.

PAM:

And maybe let me know that I'm good for something other than breakfast, lunch and dinner.

ANDREW:

You are?

PAM:

Bastard. You smell really bad.

ANDREW:

Yeah?

PAM:

You want me to run you a bath?

ANDREW:

Tigger bubble bath?

PAM:

You got it.

PAM leaves to run the bath. ANDREW sits quietly for a moment, then takes a small black book from his lunch box, then a pen. He looks over his shoulder, turns to an available page, and begins to write. Fade.

SCENE 6

At the bowling alley, GERRY and MARJORIE have just gotten their shoes.

MARJORIE:

Why *do* they make these so ugly?

GERRY:

I think it's so you don't steal them.

MARJORIE:

Funny, I think I might anyway, just because they're so bad, they're almost cool.

GERRY:

You like that word.

MARJORIE:

What word?

GERRY:

"Cool."

MARJORIE:

Yeah. It shows my lack of imagination, though, since I can't think of a better adjective.

GERRY:

You also like to talk.

MARJORIE:

Do you think that's bad?

GERRY:

No, I just noticed it.

MARJORIE:

Oh, we're already into the deconstruction phase.

GERRY:

What?

MARJORIE:

You know, we've already skipped the glamour phase when everything about me is gorgeous and sexy, and we're into the phase when you pick apart my behaviour, and find out everything that's wrong with me. Maybe we should just keep right on moving to the out-the-door phase.

GERRY:

Are you done?

MARJORIE:

Yeah.

GERRY:

Let's bowl. You can have a couple of practice shots first.

MARJORIE:

Isn't that against the rules?

GERRY:

Nah. Everyone does it.

MARJORIE:

That doesn't mean it's not against the rules.

GERRY:

Okay, you want to go up against me right now?

MARJORIE:

What an invitation. Okay, show me what to do?

GERRY:

Haven't you ever been bowling?

MARJORIE:

Not that I can remember. Not the thing in Vancouver, you know.

GERRY:

I think they play different anyway.

MARJORIE:

All I know is these don't have holes in them. Where do you put your fingers?

GERRY:

You don't. You just hold onto it.

MARJORIE:

You mean the Flintstones was all a lie?

GERRY:

Different kind of bowling. Now, just hold onto the ball, and take, like, three or four steps

She does, very slowly, without confidence.

but don't go over the line, good, now try it again, only this time, let the ball go down the lane …

She does, but their eyes follow it over …

MARJORIE:

Oh shit, sorry!

GERRY:

Actually, if you can send it down *our* lane, that would be good. Here, I'll demonstrate.

He bowls, and they watch the ball go down the lane. He gets a strike.

MARJORIE:

That was good, right?

GERRY:

That's the idea.

MARJORIE:

All right, outta my way. I'll get the hang of this.

She stands, with intense concentration, and then lets the ball go. They follow the ball with their eyes: up into the air, then down heavily.

GERRY:

(*Unable to restrain his mirth*) Well, that's an improvement. You got one.

MARJORIE:

You know, this might not be good for your own safety. I'm notoriously competitive, even when it's a lost cause.

GERRY:

I don't think that this is a lost cause. Here, I'll help you.

He goes through the motions with her.

You just have to be more fluid, not so jerky.

MARJORIE:

Who you calling jerky?

GERRY:

Just like this—see, you keep your wrist strong, so it doesn't really matter how fast you go up to the line. Then you just release …

They pause for a moment: his arms around her, she looking at him, until she notices that they knocked a few pins down.

MARJORIE:

Look I got some down!

She brushes by him, and sits, breaking the moment.

GERRY:

I'm thirsty. You want something to drink?

MARJORIE:

Sure. I don't suppose they'd have herb tea.

GERRY:

You'd suppose right.

MARJORIE:

I'll just have some of whatever you're having.

GERRY:

Okay.

He gets up to get a drink.

MARJORIE:

(*To herself*) What am I doing here? No it's all right, I can do this.

She gets up, tries to bowl on her own, but pulls a muscle.

Ow! Shit.

GERRY:

(*Returning with the drink*) Sorry! Are you all right?

MARJORIE:

Think I'll kill someone if I keep going.

GERRY:

That's okay. We can do something else. (*Pause*) Drink?

MARJORIE:

Why are you here with me? That's not what I meant. What I mean is—

GERRY:

Why aren't I married?

MARJORIE:

Something like that.

GERRY:

I don't know. I do a lot of travelling. I've been in mines all over the place. Not many women want to put up with a guy who's gone a lot.

MARJORIE:

Funny, I figure that's the easiest kind of guy *to* put up with.

GERRY:

What about you? You ever been married, or whatever?

MARJORIE:

Not married, a lot of whatever. That probably doesn't make me seem very attractive. I'm great at screwing this kind of thing up.

GERRY:

Look, we should take back these shoes. Then do you want to get a bite? There's a good Chinese restaurant, though it's probably not as good as anything you're used to.

MARJORIE:

Sounds great. I'm starved after all of that activity. You sure you have time for this?

GERRY:

I definitely have the time.

Fade.

SCENE 7

A brook in a secluded spot. A sunny fall morning. ANDREW sits on his tackle box, tying a fly to the end of his line. He seems totally contented. The spell is broken when moose calls are heard off. DAVID and GERRY enter. ANDREW stands and stares in disbelief.

ANDREW:

Gerry, what the hell are you doing?

GERRY:

Moose calls. What? What did I forget?

ANDREW:

It's not what you forgot, it's what you brought!

ANDREW points at DAVID like an inanimate object.

DAVID:

Me?

GERRY:

What's the big deal?

ANDREW:

This is the big deal! (*Gestures to the surroundings*) This spot. This *secret* spot is the big deal. You brought the Squirt to the secret spot!

GERRY:

I didn't know it was *that* secret—

DAVID:

Christ, I can go, I'll just pretend I never saw it.

ANDREW:

No, no, the damage is done. But please, guys. It took me years to find the perfect spot, and that is a once-in-a-lifetime thing. Nobody else knows but us three, okay?

DAVID:

Promise.

GERRY:

Pinky swear.

ANDREW glares at GERRY.

Okay. I swear, I promise already.

ANDREW:

Good. Now come on, the day is a-wasting.

GERRY and DAVID make for the "shore" downstage.

DAVID:

(*Shrieking*) All right! Fishy, fishy! Okay, salmon, you're going down, I'm taking you to the floor!

ANDREW:

(*In an urgent whisper*) Slowly, slowly. You don't want to spook them, dammit.

GERRY:

Should I have brought my slippers, Grampy?

ANDREW:

Don't push it, mister.

ANDREW looks down at DAVID, who is baiting his line.

What are you doing?

DAVID:

I'm baiting my line.

GERRY:

Uh-oh.

ANDREW:

You brought bait? For a fly rod? Give me that. I've been watching the water for half an hour. This is what they're going after. Here, you can use one of mine.

He hands DAVID a fly.

Have you been fly fishing before?

DAVID:

No.

ANDREW:

Didn't your dad ever take you out?

DAVID:

He died when I was little. (*Pause*) I have hand-lined before.

ANDREW:

Well, for your first time out you chose the right place. They're jumping around like crazy this morning.

Silence while they prepare to fish.

GERRY:

Southwest section started to cave in yesterday.

ANDREW:

Yeah. I heard. They sent Darryl in to get the miner out. He said the roof caved in on him all the way back to the ramp. All they cared about was the goddamn equipment. They didn't give a sweet damn if Darryl got buried or not.

DAVID:

I heard it's going to be sealed off for good.

GERRY:

Last coal we'll see for a while, then. We'll be mining for rock for the next two weeks.

ANDREW:

They'll be trying to haul us all in for overtime now. I swear they're so horny for coal they'd send us all underwater to get it.

GERRY:

Leave your phone unplugged. That's what I do ...

DAVID is attempting a very clumsy two-handed cast and is stopped just before the moment of truth.

ANDREW:

Whoa! Whoa whoa. What the hell are you doing? You're not flying a kite, man—you're *casting*. This is not just a piece of wood. In your hand, it's like a magic wand. Nice and easy. Smooth. A nice light touch. Watch me.

ANDREW centres himself. GERRY and DAVID exchange glances. ANDREW casts perfectly and sighs contentedly.

See? It has to be a part of your body. You gotta be connected. Now you try.

DAVID casts. All three look for the fly to drop in the water. It doesn't. They then look behind them in the trees. GERRY reaches up and tugs at the line.

GERRY:

You caught a birch.

ANDREW:

That's my special fly.

DAVID:

Say no more.

DAVID drops the rod and exits to climb the tree.

ANDREW:

He's a funny little guy.

GERRY:

Tough as nails.

Pause. GERRY casts.

ANDREW:

How's it going with Margie?

GERRY:

Um-hmmm.

ANDREW:

Everything's okay?

GERRY:

Yup.

Pause.

ANDREW:

You aren't going to tell me a damn thing, are you?

GERRY:

Nope.

ANDREW:

Fair enough.

DAVID:

(*Off*) Am I close?

GERRY:

(*Tugging on David's line*) You're up the wrong tree. (*Points*) That one.

ANDREW:

I wish you luck. She's an awful handful.

GERRY:

Does that mean we have your blessing?

ANDREW:

As long as you don't tell her about this spot.

GERRY:

Enough with the spot already. (*To DAVID*) Higher!

Pause.

ANDREW:

Have you ever thought about quitting?

GERRY:

You've been thinking about it, haven't you?

ANDREW:

I asked you first.

GERRY:

Yeah. I've thought about it. And then I think about welfare and I think about something else. What's the point?

ANDREW:

Those bastards don't care what happens to us, you know that. You're the one yelling at them all the time.

GERRY:

Blowing off steam and quitting are two different things. Look, is this because you gassed out—

ANDREW:

It's everything man! The cave-ins, the dust. Can you see yourself down in that hell hole ten years from now?

DAVID enters with the fly.

DAVID:

I got it.

ANDREW:

We're all proud of you, Squirt. There's some more line in the kit. This time, try putting it in the water.

Fade.

Scene 8

Pam and Andrew's kitchen. PAM is sitting, making some hot milk and honey, in her bathrobe. MARJORIE comes in from her date; her hair is undone.

MARJORIE:

Andrew's gone already?

PAM:

Yup. He's been gone for a couple of hours. I tried to go back to sleep, but once I'm up, that seems to be it.

MARJORIE:

I have the same problem.

PAM:

Do you want some Pooh milk?

MARJORIE:

Oh my God, I'd forgotten all about that.

PAM:

You probably don't drink milk, right?

MARJORIE:

Oh what the hell. One bit of milk won't kill me. Just honey though right?

PAM:

And nutmeg and cinnamon.

MARJORIE:

You've changed the recipe.

PAM:

Well, I had to make it my own ... So ... I heard the Harley, but I didn't hear you come in.

MARJORIE:

Well, Mom, it's a long walk up the steps.

PAM:

Un-hunh. How'd it go?

MARJORIE:

Well, you're the first to know. I think it might be lust.

PAM:

I thought you only liked total losers.

MARJORIE:

No, I liked artists. That's different. Besides, I figure Gerry's convertible.

PAM:

No, Gerry's motorcycle.

MARJORIE:

Jesus, too early in the morning for that.

PAM:

Look, Marjorie, I really like Gerry—

MARJORIE:

Oh God, here we go …

PAM:

Let me finish. I really like him, but I don't know if he'd be able to stick with you. He's really sweet, but he hasn't been able to keep any relationships going, at least not that I've seen.

MARJORIE:

Sounds like we're a perfect match.

PAM:

I just don't want you to think you've got a future with someone who can't see beyond his nose.

MARJORIE:

Jeez, sis, you really do like him, don't you?

PAM:

I really do, but that doesn't mean I would ever marry him, or want someone I loved to marry him.

MARJORIE:

Slow down! I had a couple of frigging dates. Besides, just because he's not with someone doesn't mean he's a loser. Not everyone gets to marry their drop-out sweetheart.

PAM:

I don't want to fight every time we talk. I'm going back to bed. Please rinse your mug out when you're done. The milk sticks.

MARJORIE:

I just wish you'd get off my back. I am capable of taking care of myself.

PAM snorts.

What the hell does that mean? You haven't been there. Look, you have your perfect man, he's got his perfect job, you've got ... your perfect house, but that doesn't mean it's right for everyone. Stop shoving your life down my throat.

PAM:

(*Wearily*) I'm not.

MARJORIE:

It sure as hell seems like you are. Everyone's got to live exactly like you do, or they don't have lives worth living.

PAM:

I just want to see you make some decisions. All I see is you wandering through life, taking whatever comes, but none of it leads anywhere. Why can't you take some responsibility?

MARJORIE:

I do. But all you remember is when I left home.

PAM:

You ran away, and for no good reason.

MARJORIE:

I didn't like it here.

PAM:

That's not a good reason to turn your back on your family.

MARJORIE:

I was sixteen. How many times do I have to apologize for—

PAM:

You said that school was out. It isn't out, and I hate it when you lie. Why won't you tell me why you're here?

MARJORIE:

It's none of your business.

PAM:

You know what? When you come crashing into my house, and eat our food, and kick my son out of his bed, it becomes my business.

MARJORIE:

Fine. I'll leave.

PAM:

Dammit, Margie, I just want to know why you're here.

MARJORIE:

You want to know why I'm here? I'm here because I had an abortion, and I needed to come home.

PAM:

(*Pause*) Oh.

MARJORIE:

I didn't think you'd like it.

PAM:

Who was the—

MARJORIE:

That's the thing, see, I'm not really sure. But, you know, it was a decision. I really did make one.

PAM:

Why didn't you call?

MARJORIE:

It's not that easy.

PAM:

No, I don't suppose it is.

MARJORIE:

Look, Pam. It's something I have to deal with on my own. I don't want to talk about it, all right?

PAM:

Fine.

MARJORIE:

Please don't tell Gerry.

PAM:

Okay. Look, I'll make you a deal. Stop picking fights with me, and I won't give you a hard time.

MARJORIE:

I'm not picking fights—

PAM catches her eye, and they laugh.

All right. Do me one more favour though? Don't go the other way and start making wedding plans.

PAM:

Deal.

Pause.

You know Andrew's job isn't perfect.

MARJORIE:

Oh, Pam, that's not going to make me feel better.

PAM:

No, really, he told me he doesn't want to be doing it anymore. He looked so worn out.

MARJORIE:

What would he do instead?

PAM:

I don't know. I just hope he doesn't do anything stupid. He's been so moody lately, and I don't know what's going on in his head. Maybe he's always been like this, and I just haven't been with him to see it. He's starting to look old, all of a sudden.

MARJORIE:

Everyone gets like that, Pam. Maybe he's just going through mid-life early.

PAM:

He'd better not, not on my time! God, it's time for Lloyd to get up.

She begins to leave, and then turns and considers MARJORIE.

Are you all right?

MARJORIE:

(*Pause*) Yeah. It's okay now … Thanks.

PAM:

Be careful. (*Business as usual*) Lloyd! Up and at 'em kiddo!

Blackout.

Scene 9

Gerry's house. There is a thumping sound from off, and then ANDREW enters, supporting GERRY.

ANDREW:

Jeez, you're awful heavy for such a little guy.

GERRY:

Everyone's little compared to you. Oh, careful.

ANDREW halts and looks around.

ANDREW:

Okay, end of the road. Where do you want to be?

GERRY:

I want to be near the TV.

ANDREW:

You know, Ger, I could actually move the TV into your bedroom.

GERRY:

Nah, my room's a mess.

ANDREW:

While this room is going to be in *Better Homes and Gardens.*

GERRY:

Yeah, well, I don't have a Pam.

ANDREW:

You got two hands buddy, and by the way, *I* do the dishes after dinner.

GERRY:

You offering your services then?

ANDREW:

No, and I'm about to let you go. I got to get back to work.

GERRY:

Okay, just help me down here.

ANDREW helps him onto the couch. GERRY is clearly in a great deal of pain. ANDREW looks on in concern.

ANDREW:

How long did they say you'd be laid up?

GERRY:

Only three days.

ANDREW:

I still don't understand why you didn't stay in the hospital.

GERRY:

I can't stand those places. I always feel like I'll come out sicker than I went in—if I come out at all. Besides I don't want to spend the money on a private room, and I don't want to share with some old geezer who's gasping for air or grabbing the nurses.

ANDREW:

If I didn't know better, I might think you were scared of them.

GERRY:

Define scared.

ANDREW:

Pissing your pants at the very idea.

GERRY:

(*Pause*) That might be a good definition. Look, I just figure I'm better at home. Besides, I'm hoping that I might get a little help.

ANDREW:

My God, you're doing the sympathy bid. You're trying to get Marjorie to feel sorry for you.

GERRY:

Nothing of the kind!

ANDREW:

You're sick!

GERRY:

No, I'm in pain. Shit.

ANDREW:

At least the beam didn't hit your head.

GERRY:

It came damn close.

ANDREW:

You have to stop complaining about everything.

GERRY:

Thanks a lot, I guess I won't be getting any sympathy from you. I did come close to dying just a little while ago, in case you hadn't noticed.

ANDREW:

No, I know. I mean complaining about the mine. That's why you're getting the shit-end of the stick.

GERRY:

At least I'm not going to gas-out anymore.

ANDREW:

No, now you get to carry steel beams in the dark. You gotta lay off the attitude. You'll get yourself killed.

GERRY:

You telling me that that piece of steel coming out of the roof and onto my back was my fault?

ANDREW:

No, of course not, but they're gonna keep giving you shit jobs until you stop giving them a hard time.

GERRY:

So if it hadn't been me, it woulda been you, or David, or one of the other guys. They don't give a shit, Andy, you said so yourself.

ANDREW:

I know, but there are better ways of changing it. You gotta bide your time. You keep telling the bosses to fuck themselves, you're just gonna dig your own grave.

GERRY:

Well at least it's better than walking into one that the company dug for me.

ANDREW:

All I'm saying is choose when to fight. You're letting your temper screw it up for you. Look I got to go. You need anything?

GERRY:

Can you just drop in at your place and let them know what happened?

ANDREW:

You want me to ask Marjorie to come over?

GERRY:

No! It's too early for that. Just let her know, and if she wants to come over, she will.

ANDREW:

Do you want me to ask her about cleaning your bedpan?

GERRY:

Slam the door on your way out, would you?

He waits for ANDREW to leave, then twists to get at the phone and phone book. Setting the phone on his lap, he leafs through it. Finding the number, he stares at it for a long while. Finally he dials.

Hi. I'd like to speak to Joseph please. Yeah, I can hold. (*As the lights fade*) Yeah, hi. My name is Gerry Hines. I work at the Westray Mine up here in Plymouth and I want to know how to lay a formal complaint.

SCENE 10

A near-empty bar on a weekday. DAVID plays a gambling machine. ANDREW enters.

DAVID:

How is he?

ANDREW:

He's okay. I dropped over before I came. I tried to get him to come along, but he just wanted to rest.

DAVID:

What did the doctor say?

ANDREW:

His back's hurt, that's for sure. They don't know how bad yet. They'll probably put him through a week's worth of tests and tell him, "Your back's hurt."

DAVID:

(*Losing a hand on the machine*) Shit.

ANDREW:

How can you plug your pay into this thing?

DAVID:

It's Gerry's fault. He got me playing them.

ANDREW:

Take my advice son, when it comes to financial planning, our friend Gerry is not your man.

DAVID:

I'm finding that out right now. Do you have—?

ANDREW:

Un-hunh, forget it. You got to learn to walk away when you're beat. (*Gives him a beer*) Drink that, it's good for ya.

Pause.

DAVID:

So, how's it been going?

ANDREW:

What, work? Same old shit. A little worse, maybe. You?

DAVID:

Pretty much the same.

ANDREW:

Oh, did I tell you about Albert? Did I tell you that yet?

DAVID:

No.

ANDREW:

Oh this is good. This is the best. I'm on the continuous miner, and everything's going okay ...

DAVID:

When was this?

ANDREW:

Ahhh ... last week, last Saturday, I think. So I'm on the miner, and things are okay, and all of a sudden there's a cave-in at the face. The machine is half covered and it's still coming down, and I'm off and running back toward the crosscut. But I catch something out of the corner of my eye. I turn, and there's Albert sitting on a gas can with a sandwich in his hand. The roof is coming down all around him, and he's still sitting there eating his sandwich! I couldn't believe my eyes. And I yelled at him, "Albert, come on, what are you waiting for!" And he looks up and says, "I like to think about things awhile before I do them." And I said, "The graveyard's full of deep thinkers, man, come on!"

DAVID:

He was just sitting there?

ANDREW:

Chewing his sandwich. By the time he moved it was all over.

DAVID:

Jesus.

ANDREW:

Can you believe it? He could have died, the stupid bugger.

Pause. ANDREW drinks.

DAVID:

Hmmm.

ANDREW:

What?

DAVID:

What?

ANDREW:

You said "hmmm" like you were hearing voices in your head.

DAVID:

I was just thinking about your story. It's funny when you think about it.

ANDREW:

I thought it was funny, and I didn't think about it.

DAVID:

There's Albert. Sitting there eating his sandwich, while the roof is falling in all around him. He could die at any moment, and he's not doing anything.

Pause.

And we both laugh at him. And we're too stupid to see that that's what we're doing.

Pause.

Funny, isn't it?

ANDREW:

You have a way of taking the piss out of a good joke, you know that? Jesus.

DAVID reaches inside his jacket and produces a folded piece of paper.

DAVID:

Have you seen this?

ANDREW takes the paper, looks at it briefly, and looks back at DAVID.

ANDREW:

You don't give up, do you?

DAVID:

There's two guys staying at the Heather right now. All I ask is that you come with me tomorrow and talk with them. It's not the same union, Andy. This is different.

ANDREW:

I don't want any trouble. I got a family to feed ...

DAVID:

Just talk to them.

ANDREW:

Who are you, Norma Rae?

DAVID:

Read that.

ANDREW begins to read.

Can I borrow a dollar?

Fade.

Scene 11

The dead of night. GERRY sits at his kitchen table in the dark, an open carton of milk on the table. He is very quiet and still. MARJORIE enters behind him, wearing GERRY's shirt.

MARJORIE:

Hey.

GERRY:

Christ, do you have to keep doing that?

MARJORIE:

What time is it?

GERRY:

I'm not sure. Pretty late, I think.

MARJORIE:

Pretty early's more like it.

She sits. GERRY takes a swig from the carton.

Have you ever heard of a glass?

GERRY:

There weren't any clean ones.

MARJORIE:

Of course.

GERRY:

I'm sorry if I woke you up. I tried not to.

MARJORIE:

It's all right.

GERRY:

(*Noticing what she's wearing*) You're settling in rather quickly, I see.

MARJORIE:

It was there. You want to play gin again?

GERRY:

No, thanks. I've been beat enough already.

MARJORIE:

Coward.

Pause. She shuffles the cards.

What's the matter?

GERRY:

Hmmm?

MARJORIE:

What's wrong? Why are we making small talk in the wee hours of the morning?

GERRY:

It's nothing, I'm having trouble sleeping, that's all.

MARJORIE:

You haven't slept through the night in four days. If your back is still bad you should go back to the doctor …

GERRY:

It's fine. It's getting better. It's the shift work, it throws off your …

MARJORIE:

Body clock.

GERRY:

Whatever.

MARJORIE:

So that's it?

GERRY:

Yeah.

Pause. MARJORIE shuffles the cards.

MARJORIE:

You talk in your sleep you know.

Pause.

I'm serious. Talk to me.

GERRY:

There's nothing to talk about. Leave me alone, will ya?

MARJORIE:

(*Quietly, firmly*) No.

Pause. GERRY sits back, looking away.

Are you okay?

GERRY:

Yeah, I'm all right.

MARJORIE:

I don't believe you.

They look at each other.

Please don't lie to me.

Pause.

GERRY:

Every night. Every night it's the same. I wake up, and the phone is ringing. It all happens like slow motion, like I'm underwater. I know that I have to get to the phone, that it's so important that I get this call, and I'm running down the hall, and it's ringing louder and louder, and I reach out to pick it up ... and just before I touch it, it explodes, and everything goes white. And I'm too late.

Pause.

And then I wake up all over again. It's going to be real, someday. I know it. One day I'll pick up the phone and somebody on the other end is going to tell me they're all gone. And I'm too late.

MARJORIE:

It's that bad?

GERRY:

It's that bad.

MARJORIE:

(*Firmly*) So you'll leave.

GERRY:

Don't be stupid. I am not going on welfare.

MARJORIE:

There are better jobs, Gerry.

GERRY:

This is all I know!

MARJORIE:

You have to do something.

Pause.

GERRY:

I *have* done something. After my doctor's appointment on Thursday, I went to the Department of Labour. I know a guy there, Joseph. I knew him at Gays River. I talked to him and two other guys for almost three hours. They couldn't believe the stuff I was telling them. People gassing out, the cave-ins, everything. Joey filled a whole pad of paper writing it all down. They said I was the first person to go on record, to make a complaint.

MARJORIE:

So what happens now?

GERRY:

They close it down until it's safe. I'm surprised they didn't do it yesterday. I'm supposed to meet Joey at the Heather tomorrow afternoon. I guess I have to sign something.

Pause.

Why are you looking at me like that?

MARJORIE:

Because.

GERRY:

For God's sake don't tell anyone. Not even Pam. Not yet. If I want the whole town to know, I'll hire a blimp.

GERRY makes his way to bed.

MARJORIE:

Gerry?

GERRY:

Yeah.

MARJORIE:

Will they close it before you have to go back down?

GERRY:

I don't know. I hope so.

He exits.

MARJORIE:

I hope so too.

She takes a swig from the carton. Fade.

Scene 12

Evening. Pam and Andrew's dining room. DAVID and ANDREW sit at the table, playing cards.

ANDREW:

If he doesn't show up with that food soon I'm going to start eating you. Eights?

DAVID:

Go fish. Did he say anything on the phone?

ANDREW:

No. Don't forget, we're not supposed to know. If he brings it up, fine. Otherwise, play dumb.

DAVID:

Do my best. Fours?

ANDREW:

Ahhhh!

He hands them over.

GERRY:

(*Off*) Hi!

GERRY enters carrying boxes of doughnuts and junk food. He is subdued.

ANDREW:

Finally. Where the hell were you, getting a massage?

GERRY:

I think I've got everything ... this is for you ...

DAVID:

Thank God you came when you did. Cannibalism was becoming a big possibility.

GERRY:

Remind me never to go camping with you guys. This is yours ...

ANDREW:

Assorted?

GERRY:

Only the best. You can fight over the other stuff.

DAVID:

Where's Marjorie?

GERRY:

She's out shopping with Pam somewhere.

ANDREW:

(*Casually*) You know, I think it's great that you and Marjorie have been getting along so well.

GERRY:

Really?

ANDREW:

Of course. Since you've been going out with her, we don't see her around here at all. It's beautiful.

DAVID:

How's the back?

GERRY:

It's okay. I'll probably have to keep working up top, though. They won't let me rest long enough to get back underground.

ANDREW:

You'll get better. Take advantage of it while you can. Are we gonna talk or play crib?

DAVID:

(*Quickly*) Hairpins.

ANDREW:

Matches.

GERRY:

That leaves … toothpicks. Where did all the pegs go, anyway?

ANDREW:

Lloyd swallowed them all. I think they're still in him. Cut for deal.

ANDREW wins cut.

So what's new, anyway?

GERRY:

Not much.

DAVID:

No news to report?

GERRY:

Nope.

ANDREW:

Well, I guess we'll all have to try and contain our excitement.

GERRY:

Okay …

Silence as they all consider their cards. DAVID discards immediately, and fidgets. ANDREW and DAVID rearrange their hands.

DAVID:

So, are they going to close it down?

ANDREW:

(*Throwing his cards down on the table*) Christ!

GERRY:

What?

ANDREW:

(*To DAVID*) I said *play* dumb, not *be* dumb!

GERRY:

(*Concerned*) What's going on?

Pause.

DAVID:

We know you went to the Labour Department and complained … and we know you had a meeting with the inspector.

GERRY:

Does this mean that all the guys know? Does everyone know this?

Pause. DAVID and ANDREW look at each other, and then down.

I see. Well, it's true. I met with Joey yesterday.

ANDREW:

So? What are they going to do?

GERRY:

Well, I met him at the Heather. I said we could meet somewhere for coffee, but he wanted to meet at his room. He said we could talk there. So I show up, and he answers the door, and he looks like he's going to a funeral. I sit down on the bed, and he turns the TV up really loud so nobody could hear what we were saying. He said that I had two choices. If he put in a good word for me at Westray, and I kept my mouth shut, I might keep my job—if I was lucky. Or, I could walk the street. That's just how he said it, too. "You can walk the street with the rest of them."

DAVID:

He didn't believe you?

GERRY:

Oh, he believed me. He said so. They believed everything. But the official word is that the mine is safe. And if the mine is safe, I have no grounds for complaint. I couldn't believe what I was hearing, and I kept trying to turn the TV down, but he kept turning it back up again. I said, "How can you believe me and say it's safe?" He just looked at me and said, "You've got to make a choice." And then he said, "This meeting never happened." So I left.

Pause.

DAVID:

That's it?

GERRY:

That's all.

Pause.

ANDREW:

Gerry, on our days off, David and I are gonna be signing up people in the parking lot for the union drive. It would be a big help if you would be there with us.

GERRY:

You're working for the union?

ANDREW:

I just signed up.

GERRY:

When?

DAVID:

About thirty seconds ago, apparently.

GERRY:

There must be something in these doughnuts.

ANDREW:

What do you say?

Pause.

GERRY:

You bring the coffee, I'll be there. (*GERRY discards*) Your crib.

ANDREW:

Oh, yeah. I forgot.

He collects his hand, considering it.

You know, I was thinking yesterday, during the shift change, that hardly a minute goes by without somebody we know working down there. I was watching the boys go down—I know most of them, you know? And I thought ... when something happens ... Christ, between Davey and I, that's a fifty-fifty chance one of us is going to be down there. I mean, what do you hope for?

I want you to promise me something, Gerry. If one of us is down there when all hell breaks loose, you go public with it. You tell everybody everything you know, right away. I'm talking newspapers, TV, you name it. Don't wait for them to cover everything over. Don't wait for anything. If I die down there, I don't want those bastards to get away with it. I want you to promise me that. Okay?

Pause.

GERRY:

I promise.

ANDREW:

Good. I need a beer.

He gets up and exits for the beer.

GERRY:

Well, guys, I want to thank you for a wonderful relaxing evening. I have never been so thoroughly depressed since Denver blew the Superbowl.

DAVID:

Which one?

GERRY:

Ha-ha.

Re-entering, ANDREW hands a bottle of beer to each of them.

ANDREW:

I propose a toast, gentlemen.

GERRY:

What's the occasion?

ANDREW:

Being here.

Bottles clink. Fade.

Scene 13

Pam and Andrew's dining room. Things are in an absolute fury. PAM and MARJORIE are decorating a cake, and GERRY is standing around.

PAM:

What do you think? Smarties for the nose?

MARJORIE:

No, no, it's got to be a gummy bear nose.

GERRY:

How about a jelly tot?

The women look at him.

Sorry. Well, how about stickin' one of them licorice cigars in his mouth?

MARJORIE:

Yes dear, that's a brilliant idea.

GERRY:

Where's Andy?

PAM:

He's upstairs. Lloyd took a fit when I said that he had to go to sleep, so his dad's giving him a talking to.

MARJORIE:

He must be really excited.

PAM:

You don't know the half of it. He knows we're up to something down here, but he doesn't have any idea what.

MARJORIE:

Ger, as long as you're sitting, get busy. You're in the wrapping business.

He reaches for a present to wrap.

GERRY:

What the hell is this one?

MARJORIE:

Here, here, let me show you. Something perfect for every little boy.

She shows him "The Flubber," which makes a rude noise.

PAM:

Oh my God, you're giving *that* to Lloyd?

MARJORIE:

Yeah, what's wrong with it? I think it's great.

GERRY:

I love it.

ANDREW comes down the stairs, catches the noise.

ANDREW:

What the hell was that?

GERRY makes a "Flubber" noise.

Everything pretty much set?

PAM:

Well, we may be up most of the night, but we'll get it done. How's Lloyd?

ANDREW:

Proud as anything. I told him where we're going tomorrow.

PAM:

Oh Andrew, I wanted it to be a surprise for him.

ANDREW:

It was going to be, but, it was the only way that I could get him to stop bouncing off the walls.

GERRY:

Where *are* you taking him tomorrow?

ANDREW:

I'm taking him to the spot.

GERRY:

The spot?

ANDREW:

Uh-huh.

MARJORIE:

For the first time?

ANDREW:

Uh-huh. And it's just him and me. We'll be back in time to barbecue whatever we catch for the party.

PAM:

(*To MARJORIE*) I've got hamburgers just in case.

ANDREW:

Oh, it's nice to see how much faith my own wife has in me.

PAM:

Oh, guess what? I even found something for you to eat: "tofu dogs."

GERRY:

There enough for two of us?

PAM:

Sure, if you want them.

ANDREW:

Oh, Gerry, come on, not you too. I got to have some support around here, buddy.

GERRY:

Don't worry, just something to make my love feel included.

MARJORIE and GERRY make kissy faces at PAM and ANDREW.

ANDREW:

Yuck. Okay, I'm out of here.

PAM:

Lloyd is okay though? I don't need to check on him?

ANDREW:

Nope. I told him that I needed him to be more responsible now that he was going to be six, and that I expected him to be the man of the house from now on. That made him puff right up. That was part of the deal for showing him the spot.

GERRY:

Think he'll keep the secret?

ANDREW:

He knows what I'll do if he doesn't. I'm off.

GERRY:

How you gonna go to the spot if you're working all night tonight?

ANDREW:

I'll catch a few winks in the morning.

GERRY:

Why don't you just skip it?

ANDREW:

What, the whole shift?

GERRY:

Yeah, what the hell. You could give us a hand, that way Pam can't keep us slaving away all night.

PAM:

Who you think is paying for all these presents? Oh listen, before I forget, are you gonna see David down there?

ANDREW:

Probably. If he didn't get off early, and if you'd actually let me get out the door.

PAM:

You should invite him to the party.

ANDREW:

Jeez. He gets invited everywhere these days.

MARJORIE:

I think he's lonely. When he heard us talking about the party before, he looked like his puppy'd been run over.

ANDREW:

All right, no problem. (*Takes PAM aside*) Take care tonight.

PAM:

You too, baby.

ANDREW:

I love you.

PAM:

Yeah, yeah, we're married, remember?

ANDREW:

I mean it Pam. I really do, you know?

PAM:

(*Pause*) I know. I love you too. Oh, ring.

She puts out her hand.

ANDREW:

No, that's okay. I want to wear it. See you.

He waves to the others, and exits. PAM stands there. Pause.

MARJORIE:

You okay?

PAM:

What? Yeah … yeah. I'm fine.

She moves back to the table.

Gerry! What did you do to the bear?

GERRY:

I gave him a stogie.

MARJORIE takes the cigar out of the cake and shoves it in GERRY's mouth. Fade.

SCENE 14

A locker room at Westray. ANDREW is getting ready to go down. DAVID enters from the previous shift carrying a lunch box. DAVID is drained.

ANDREW:

Hey, Squirt. You're off a bit early, aren't ya?

DAVID:

Few minutes.

ANDREW:

You look like shit warmed over.

DAVID:

Thanks. (*Pause*) Andy, it's bad down there today. I'd blow it off if I were you.

ANDREW:

Why?

DAVID:

A couple of guys gassed out. It's dusty as hell down there.

ANDREW:

In other words, a typical day at work.

DAVID:

I heard the sniffer on the continuous is busted. This is the worst I've ever seen it. I'm not kidding.

ANDREW:

I'm sure you're right, Squirt, but there isn't much I can do about that, is there? I like to keep my sick days for fishing, anyway.

DAVID:

It's Lloyd's birthday tomorrow, isn't it?

ANDREW:

Yup. I'm taking him to the spot.

DAVID:

Whoa. That's quite a present.

ANDREW:

Yeah. He already knows. I never could keep a secret from him. He almost peed his pants when I told him … Shit.

DAVID:

What's up?

ANDREW:

I forgot my lunch.

DAVID:

Here. Take mine. I never stopped long enough to eat it anyway.

DAVID hands his lunch box to ANDREW.

ANDREW:

Right on. What you got?

DAVID:

I don't remember.

ANDREW:

It doesn't matter. I won't get a chance to eat it either. Maybe we can just keep passing the same lunch back and forth every day. We'd save a pile of money.

Pause. He gets his gear on.

Tell you what. You come along to the party tomorrow.

DAVID:

No, I don't want to …

ANDREW:

Stop. You're so polite sometimes you make me sick. Lloyd likes you. You make him laugh. You sure as hell make me laugh.

DAVID:

Okay.

Pause. ANDREW finishes getting ready.

Hey, Andy, it's only one shift.

ANDREW:

It isn't just one shift, it's a lot more than that. If I run scared today, how do I know I can go back down there tomorrow? I can't second guess myself every time I tape up my boots. It's the only way I can do it. So. I'll see ya, Squirt.

DAVID:

See ya.

ANDREW exits. Fade on DAVID, as he takes off his boots.

Scene 15

Darkness. Silence. A phone rings three times. On the fourth ring, we see PAM in a small pool of light. She is in her nightclothes.

PAM:

Hello? Yes? Yes it is. No he's at work, who is this?

Another pool of light. DAVID answers the phone.

DAVID:

Hello? What? Yeah, who's this?

PAM:

What? What time is it?

DAVID:

It's six thirty in the morning, where the hell else would I be?

PAM:

What? What do you mean?

DAVID:

(*Pause*) What?

PAM:

Why, what happened?

Another pool of light. GERRY in nightclothes.

GERRY:

(*Out of breath*) Hello!

PAM:

Where is that?

DAVID:

Oh God. I'm on my way.

DAVID hangs up and runs out of the light.

PAM:

All right, I'll be there as soon as I—

GERRY:

Yeah, who's this?

PAM:

Hello?

GERRY:

When?

PAM:

Hello!

She hangs up and runs out of the light. Pause.

GERRY:

I'll be right there.

GERRY hangs up. MARJORIE comes beside him, eyes full of sleep, takes the receiver from his hand.

MARJORIE:

What's going on?

GERRY stands still, entranced.

GERRY:

It's real. (*Pause*) This time it's real.

Blackout.

Scene 16

At the firehall, PAM sits behind a table wearing Andy's jacket. MARJORIE walks over with a cup of coffee.

MARJORIE:

Here.

PAM doesn't respond.

Pam, please, you have to have something.

PAM shakes her head.

Look, they told us that it would be a while. I called Lloyd's sitter and told her to keep the TV off. Is there anything else I should have told her?

PAM:

She'll be fine.

MARJORIE:

Okay.

Silence. DAVID walks in, and gestures to MARJORIE. She gets up, goes over to him, and hands him a coffee.

What's going on out there?

DAVID:

It's nuts. There are reporters from all over the place. Every time you walk anywhere near their hall, they just maul you.

MARJORIE:

Is there any more word?

DAVID:

No, but the last team hasn't come up yet. Jesus, they're still trying to figure out who's down there.

MARJORIE:

What do you mean?

DAVID:

Why do you think they called everybody this morning? They didn't even have a clue who was working.

MARJORIE:

David, what does it look like down there?

Pause.

DAVID:

What do you mean?

MARJORIE:

How bad is it?

DAVID:

We're not supposed to say.

MARJORIE:

Jesus, David ...

DAVID:

It's not good.

Pause.

Listen, Gerry asked me to come talk to you.

MARJORIE:

Why? What is it?

DAVID:

He's going down with the next draeger team—

MARJORIE:

What?

DAVID:

He's getting suited up right now.

MARJORIE:

What about his back?

DAVID:

He says he can manage it.

MARJORIE:

Can't they do without him?

DAVID:

He knows the mine. The Devco guys don't. I'm going back down with him in a minute to meet the new team. (*Pause*) Marjorie, he'll be okay. He knows what he's doing. I gotta go. (*Pause*) You all right?

MARJORIE:

Yeah, I just want them to be okay.

DAVID:

(*Shrugs*) Yeah, me too.

He exits quickly, while MARJORIE is looking away.

MARJORIE:

(*Goes back to PAM*) Well, this must set a record for the number of coffees wasted.

She grabs PAM's cup, and starts playing with it.

Do you find it hot in here? I wonder what it's like out in Vancouver now. I did miss it here when I went out west. You probably won't believe me, but I hung out with almost no one but Maritimers. You wonder what the point is of moving so far away when the only people you see remind you constantly of home. (*Pause*) Pam, I wish you'd talk to me ... You're like my old boyfriends. What are you thinking? Nothing. How do so many men get dressed, much less drive a car, without thinking? My brain just keeps going all the time—

PAM:

So does your mouth.

MARJORIE:

Yeah. Sorry.

PAM:

Don't be sorry, just shut up.

MARJORIE:

Okay.

Fade.

SCENE 17

The firehall. PAM and MARJORIE are in different poses than before. PAM is still in the chair, and her leg is twitching.

PAM:

Why won't something happen?

MARJORIE:

We should know something soon …

PAM:

You keep saying that.

GERRY enters.

Gerry, what's going on? Have you seen him?

GERRY:

No, Pam. It's going to take more time.

PAM:

Why? What's taking so long?

MARJORIE:

Pam, they're working as fast as they can.

GERRY:

We don't know anything yet. As soon as I hear something you'll be the first to know. I promise.

PAM:

I can't stand this, Gerry. No one tells me anything.

GERRY:

As soon as I know anything, I promise. Marjorie, can I see you? I'm just going to talk to your sister for a sec, Pam. Okay?

PAM nods. GERRY guides MARJORIE away.

MARJORIE:

Are you all right? Jesus, Gerry, you look awful. Are you going back down?

GERRY:

No. I'm through. I told them I can't do it anymore. The roof is looking worse every time.

MARJORIE:

How's David doing? Is he still down there?

GERRY:

(*Long pause*) Margie …

MARJORIE:

What?

GERRY:

They've found some of the boys. They're dead. Eleven of them … I saw some of them … Jesus, they're burned all to shit. (*Breaks down*) They're all gone. There's no way anyone's still alive. I'm sorry.

MARJORIE:

You lied to her.

GERRY:

What am I supposed to do?

Pause.

MARJORIE:

Is Andrew there?

GERRY:

I don't know. The next team's bagging them, and they're taking them to the morgue. David's going to try to identify—

MARJORIE:

Who's gonna tell Pam? Do we just wait until the company decides to tell us?

GERRY:

Right now we have to. Look I don't know if Andrew's in that group. Maybe he is still alive. I don't … I just can't do it. I know it's cold, but I'm not risking my life to carry dead bodies. I don't want to see him.

MARJORIE:

What do we do now?

GERRY:

We wait. I'll see you soon.

MARJORIE:

I love you.

GERRY touches her face, then turns and leaves. MARJORIE turns, and finally screws up the courage to face her sister. She sits parallel to her sister, on the opposite side of the table.

PAM:

(*Still sitting. Pause.*) What did he tell you?

MARJORIE:

(*Pause*) Nothing ... He's really tired. I think his back is giving out on him, so he's going to go back to his place and lie down for a bit.

PAM:

His *back* hurts?

MARJORIE:

Pam, everyone's doing everything they can.

Pause.

PAM:

I know.

Both stay in their chairs, facing front, slumping. Fade.

Scene 18

The firehall. A few hours later. PAM is sitting still in the same chair, and she is leaning on the table, possibly asleep. MARJORIE is pacing, trying to stay awake. GERRY, in a new shirt, comes in, and MARJORIE quickly goes over to him.

MARJORIE:

Any news?

GERRY:

(*Shakes his head*) Should be coming soon. Look, we can wait here, for the official announcement, or we can wait for David outside, and try and get it out there. This place is nuts.

MARJORIE:

I know, but I can't get Pam to even stand up. Now she thinks that as long as she stays on that chair—that Andrew's okay.

GERRY:

Jesus.

MARJORIE:

There's no hope?

GERRY shrugs.

Well, of course there has to be some, after all the guys in Springhill lived for days.

GERRY:

That was a different mine.

MARJORIE:

I know.

DAVID walks in, and nods to GERRY.

GERRY:

Marjorie, we should get Pam out of here now.

MARJORIE:

Oh God.

She walks over to PAM, kneels in front of her, and touches her knee.

Pam—

PAM:

(*Waking immediately*) What happened? What's going on?

MARJORIE:

(*Still kneeling*) Pam, we should go outside for a second.

PAM:

No. I don't want to leave.

GERRY:

Pam …

DAVID steps forward, looking absolutely miserable. He is obviously exhausted.

DAVID:

Pam, I saw Andrew.

PAM:

You saw him? Is he at the hospital? Can I—

GERRY:

Pam, when I went down my last time, we found eleven guys. They're dead. David had to do the identification he just—

Pause.

Andy's dead.

Pause. PAM looks from GERRY to DAVID, then finally to MARJORIE, who tries to touch her.

MARJORIE:

I am so sorry—

PAM:

(*Rising away from the three*) No!

Pause.

MARJORIE:

Oh, God, Pam, I'm sorry.

PAM just stares, then starts to break down, finally collapsing into MARJORIE's arms.

We should get her out of here now.

GERRY takes PAM, and supports her out.

DAVID:

They're going to make the announcement soon.

MARJORIE:

David, thank you.

DAVID:

(*Bitterly*) For what?

MARJORIE:

For making sure.

DAVID exits. MARJORIE collects PAM's things, including Andy's jacket, which PAM had been wearing, then exits.

Scene 19

A locker room at Westray. DAVID has just arrived, taking off his coat and gear.

GERRY:

Anything?

DAVID:

It's slow. A lot of water. Last crew down saw smoke. It looks bad.

GERRY:

Listen, we should talk. Take a look at this.

GERRY gives a small black book to DAVID.

DAVID:

What's this?

GERRY:

Read it. It was in Andy's truck, he left it behind before the shift.

DAVID:

It's a diary?

GERRY:

Every shift he worked, he logged an entry. Everything that he saw that wasn't right, he wrote it down. There's even diagrams in there.

DAVID:

I never heard him talk about this.

GERRY:

Nobody did. Not even Pam.

DAVID:

None of this seems real.

GERRY:

Listen, I'm talking to a TV reporter today. I want you to come too.

Pause.

DAVID:

What?

GERRY:

A guy from the CBC is going to meet me at my place at three.

DAVID:

Today? You're going on TV today? You must be joking.

GERRY:

You were here, you heard Andy. When something happens, we go public. No waiting.

DAVID:

What are you going to say?

GERRY:

Everything.

DAVID:

There are draegermen still down there, Gerry. What about the families? We don't even know if the other guys are alive or dead, and you're going on the TV to tell everybody the place is a deathtrap?

GERRY:

I'm doing it for those guys. You think any of them would want me to keep quiet and give the company time to cover its tracks? Why do you think they're telling us not to talk to any reporters?

DAVID:

Have you cleared this with the union?

GERRY:

Why, David? Why do I need permission to tell the truth?

DAVID:

Because some of us would like to have a job when this is all over.

Pause. DAVID sits.

GERRY:

My God. That's what this is all about, isn't it? You're scared they'll close the mine if I tell the truth.

DAVID:

I have nothing to be—

GERRY:

You're not worried about anybody else but yourself. Are you? I made a promise. I made a promise to Andy that I have to keep. I don't give a damn if it hurts, or if it upsets people or if it's convenient for anybody. Andy only ever asked me for one favour and I'm sure as hell not going to back out on him now. (*Pause*) I would have done the same for you.

GERRY grabs his coat and puts it on.

Are you with me?

Pause. Silence. DAVID looks at the book, then gives it back to GERRY without looking at him. GERRY takes the book and exits. Fade.

Scene 20

Pam and Andrew's house. PAM is fully dressed. She clutches a cup of tea. MARJORIE enters.

MARJORIE:

You're up.

PAM:

Un-hunh.

MARJORIE:

Did you sleep?

PAM:

I don't know if you'd call it sleep.

MARJORIE:

Is there anything you need?

PAM:

No.

MARJORIE:

Where's Lloyd?

PAM:

He's riding his bike out back.

MARJORIE:

Look, Pam, I know it is hard right now, but you're going to have to talk to him about all of this. He's—

PAM:

I already did.

MARJORIE:

How did he take it?

PAM:

He'll live.

MARJORIE:

He'll live? Pam, I know they're offering counselling, but I have the names of a couple of—

PAM:

Stop it. I know how to raise my own son.

MARJORIE:

I just think this is different from wetting the bed.

GERRY comes in, unseen by PAM.

PAM:

You don't know anything at all.

MARJORIE:

Pam, I—

PAM:

(*Finally explodes*) No! I am not interested in hearing parenting theories from someone whose only experience is an aborted baby.

Pause. MARJORIE looks from PAM to GERRY.

MARJORIE:

I … I have to go.

GERRY:

No, don't.

He goes to her, and takes her arm. Pause. PAM notices that GERRY is there.

PAM:

Why not? She'll be gone as soon as she gets bored anyway.

MARJORIE breaks from GERRY, moving forward.

GERRY:

Pam, you're not being fair.

PAM:

Fair? You want to talk to me about fair? If you're looking for forgiveness, you won't find it here.

GERRY:

What do you mean?

PAM:

Don't treat me like an idiot. Did you really think the TV would be off forever?

Pause.

I woke up, came downstairs, and thought I'd skip right quick to a soap, but the first thing I saw was your face on the six o'clock news. (*To MARJORIE*) Five whole minutes of Gerry telling the world how dangerous it was to work at Westray. Every day you were risking your life down there, he said. Everybody knew this was going to happen.

The place was a deathtrap, and everybody knew except me. Every day, I rolled him out of bed, packed his lunch, and sent him on his way, and everybody knew. Everybody knew.

Pause.

(*To GERRY*) Margie. Andy. You. And I find out on the six o'clock news.

GERRY:

Pam, I didn't have a choice.

PAM:

You knew. You knew that it was going to blow up and you kept that from me. Andy was my husband. We weren't amateurs at this, we were in it for life. How can I be the last to know?

Pause.

I sent him down there, I told him not to quit, and nobody told me the truth. Can you explain that to me? Because if you can, maybe you can explain it to a little boy who doesn't understand why his Daddy won't come home. Then maybe we'll both understand.

MARJORIE:

I think maybe everyone just wanted to protect you.

PAM:

So who's going to protect me now?

Fade.

SCENE 21

Outside Pam and Andrew's house. A beautiful day, after the funeral. MARJORIE is throwing bread to the birds.

MARJORIE:

This is not for you, you big bully.

DAVID comes up to her.

Hi.

DAVID:

Hi.

MARJORIE:

You look a bit more rested than the last time I saw you.

DAVID:

Well, the doc gave me a couple of pills, and told me to unplug the phone. There wasn't anything more to do anyway.

MARJORIE:

Have a seat. You want a cup of coffee?

DAVID:

No, thanks.

Pause. MARJORIE throws some more bread at the birds.

MARJORIE:

Oh, I hate seagulls. They're such pigs.

DAVID:

(*Pause*) How was the funeral?

MARJORIE:

It was good. I don't know. What the hell are you supposed to say about them? I guess it was nice.

DAVID:

That's good.

MARJORIE:

Why didn't you come?

DAVID:

I was going to, but I thought I should let it be for a while.

MARJORIE:

You had as much a right to be there as anyone.

DAVID:

How's Lloyd?

MARJORIE:

This morning, when he woke up—he said that he'd never be able to go fishing now, because his Dad knew all the best spots.

DAVID:

I could take him sometime.

MARJORIE:

That's a nice offer. I don't think Pam would understand right now.

DAVID:

How is she?

MARJORIE:

Up and down. Things set her off, everybody has to clear out. She got Andy's union card in the mail yesterday.

DAVID:

At least they can help look after her now.

MARJORIE:

Yeah. I guess.

DAVID:

Marjorie, how's Gerry doing?

MARJORIE:

He's all right. He went down again with the Mounties. I don't know if he'll ever go underground again.

DAVID:

I just wondered, you know, if—

MARJORIE:

Look David, why don't you just go and talk with him?

DAVID:

I'm not sure he'd want to see me.

MARJORIE:

Since the interviews, his calendar's been pretty open.

DAVID:

He doesn't understand why I said no.

MARJORIE:

You make your own choices, you know?

Pause.

I have something that belongs to you. Gerry found it when he went down with the Mounties. Just a sec.

She goes into the house and retrieves a battered lunch box, then offers it to David.

You must have left it there on your last shift. I don't know if you would want it anymore. You must have left it down there on your last shift—

DAVID:

No, no I gave it to him.

MARJORIE:

What?

DAVID:

To Andy. I gave it to Andy, that last shift change. He said he forgot his lunch, and I hadn't eaten mine, so I gave it to him. It was next to him. He had it next to him when he died. I can't …

MARJORIE:

Oh, David, I'm so sorry.

During this monologue, PAM comes up distantly behind them, dressed in her widow's weeds. She can hear them, but they don't notice her.

DAVID:

No, no, I am. I knew what it was like down there, I knew what would happen. I could feel that it was wrong, but I let him go down. I even gave him my fucking lunch, and now he's gone, and I didn't do anything about it. Jesus, I didn't even have the guts to speak out about it … Do you know what it's like to feel like you're gonna go to hell, but you can't do the one thing that might save you? I saw him, I saw him afterwards, I looked at him, and he was so burned up. You know I still can't close my eyes without seeing the faces—Andy's and all the others from the morgue, face after face after face. But when I looked down at him, this guy who's done everything for me, all I could think was that it could have been me, and I was so fucking glad that it wasn't me, and I know that Pam must be able to see that. She's lost everything, and I was happy for me, happy that I was looking down at Andy, and it wasn't the other way around. And I got mad. He'd been mining for years. I need a job so bad, and all I could think was that he should have fucking known better.

PAM:

You're right.

DAVID:

Pam, I didn't want you—

PAM:

No, he *should* have known better. I thought I should have known, but how could I? He was down there, and I wasn't. It's not your fault, David, any more than it was his.

Pause.

Look, I'm not mad at you, but you have to stop treating me like I'm some sort of goddamned saint. I'm a Westray Widow. I'll always be that, but I have a name. It's Pam, and I have to figure out who that is now on my own, 'cause the biggest part of who I was is dead and buried. I may ask for help, or I may not, but if you want to be around me, you're all going to have to treat me like I'm still alive.

MARJORIE:

Okay.

DAVID:

Um, okay.

Pause.

PAM:

Well, it's been a long day. Let's have a beer.

Fade.

Scene 22

The secret spot. One year later. Warm sunshine. PAM sits near the shore, her face turned up to the sun. GERRY is showing MARJORIE how to cast. DAVID is casting as well, only now with great ease and concentration.

GERRY:

That's it. That was a lot farther.

MARJORIE:

This is crazy.

GERRY:

You'll get the hang of it. Look at him. First time I brought him up here he caught a tree.

PAM:

This is a lovely spot. Thank you.

GERRY:

Where's the birthday boy?

DAVID:

He's just down there. (*Pointing down river*) See?

PAM:

He's getting awfully far. I should go get him …

MARJORIE:

No, you sit. Here Gerry, hold this. I'll bound after him. It'll get me in practice.

She runs off stage left.

Lloyd? Lloyd!

PAM:

She's going to be a great mom.

GERRY:

I think we'll do okay.

PAM:

It's such a relief to see her so happy.

Pause.

Thanks for being with me today. It means a lot.

DAVID:

I can't think of anywhere else I would rather be.

GERRY:

Me too. Although I would like it better if the trout were biting.

PAM:

Don't worry, I've got hamburgers just in case. I've got something for you guys.

DAVID:

For us?

PAM:

Yup. In the cooler here.

She removes a bottle of wine.

Do you recognize this? (*No response*) It's the wine that they gave out at the opening of the mine, do you remember? Andy stole a bottle at the reception and brought it home. Give us your jackknife, Gerry. We were saving it for when the house was paid off. When we burned the mortgage we were going to have a romantic dinner, and break open this wine and celebrate. Andy would be retired, and we'd have years ahead of us.

She opens the bottle and pours into little plastic glasses.

So many times I've thought about going up to the mine and smashing this bottle across the goddamn towers. Once, in the middle of the night, I actually got out of bed, got in the car and started off to do it.

Well, the insurance has paid the house off now, and I don't like to drink by myself. I think Andy would have wanted it this way, don't you?

She hands DAVID and GERRY each a glass.

To the secret spot.

PAM drinks. The others don't.

A whole year. My whole life changed in that one night and a year later nothing has changed. That's so strange, isn't it?

Pause.

I close my eyes, sometimes, to see his face. To make me feel better. When the house is cold and I feel alone.

Pause.

I can't see his face anymore, Gerry. I can't see it.

GERRY:

I know.

PAM:

Gerry, don't ever let them make you feel bad for talking when you did. Andy would be proud of you.

GERRY:

I know, Pam.

PAM:

Don't let them forget. Either of you. Don't you dare.

GERRY:

Okay.

Pause.

PAM:

Don't tell anyone about this spot, okay?

GERRY:

Okay.

Fade to black. Curtain.